FutureWord Publishing

©2013 Mary A. Scobey All Rights Reserved.
The Trials and Triumphs of Growing Older
ISBN13:978-0615905914
ISBN-10: 0615905919
First Print Edition: 11.22.13
Second Print Edition: 09/05/14
Cover art by Carol Caudle
Clipart from Microsoft
Photo images and rose drawings by Mary Scobey

This is a non-fiction book based, in part, on incidences in the life of Mary Ashmore Scobey. No part of this book may be reproduced, stored in a retrieval system, or transmitted by any means, electronic, mechanical, photocopying, recording, or otherwise, without written permission from the author and the publisher.

www.futureword.net

Requests for speaking or signing events should be directed to : FutureWord Publishing, 384 Goodman Rd. E. Ste. 210, Southaven, MS 38671 Fax 217-8514

ACKNOWLEDGEMENTS

My sincere appreciation goes to Cheryl Haynes, FutureWord Publishing Executive, without whose guidance and encouragement this little book could not have been published. Accolades to Carol Caudle, whose sketch of me blowing out eighty-eight birthday candles graces the cover. Her talent is amazing. Many thanks are due to my sweet husband whose dinner was late many evenings while I typed my stories, and to my son, Gene Scobey, Jr. and daughter, Julianne Parks, thank you so much for all your help in gathering photos to illustrate my stories. Last, but not least, much love to our grandson, William, who patiently posed with his little cars parked in his mother's dollhouse, for a picture to accompany his story. Thank you, thank you, each and every one!

INTRODUCTION

It is my hope that those of you in the prime of life will find the stories in this little book inspirational and informative as well as sometimes amusing, and for those of you, who have reached their senior years, let's commiserate. I make no claims of being a geriatric specialist, but from the advanced age of eighty-eight, I want to share with you the various pro's and con's I have experienced in living to a ripe old age. I am aware that some of you have different experiences from mine but, no doubt, there are many which are similar. I often say "been there – done that" when someone shares a senior incident with me. I can certainly relate.

Statistics prove that age expectancy increases each year we live due to medical breakthrough and technology, and I hear more and more of some who have reached the century mark and are living productive lives. Just recently I attended a birthday party for ninety year-old twins and was amazed at their sharp wit and agility. Their beautiful smiles and graciousness reflect their enthusiasm for life. Certainly life is not over when you reach retirement. Far from it. Some of your best days lie ahead.

Of course in most every life there are some trials along the way, but the triumphs far exceed the trials. I couldn't agree more than with the philosophical quote by Marilynne Robinson in *Gilead:* "There are a thousand, thousand reasons to live this life and every one of them sufficient." And so there are!

Enjoy –
Mary A. Scobey

The Trials and Triumphs of Growing Older

Mary Ashmore Scobey

OLD! WHO, ME?

For some years now, I've been aware that old age was out there somewhere but definitely somewhere in the future. Not yet, I'd tell myself while in my seventies… but maybe when I reach that eightieth birthday. Besides, isn't age a relative thing? A mental attitude? I've known people in their forties who were old. But then the big eight-oh kind-of sneaked up on me, and I wailed to my husband, "But I don't want to be old!" Gene, my husband, who is a very sensible, practical man replied, "Just think of the alternative." That shut me up real fast. But still, I couldn't delay it any longer. Old age had caught up with me. Always one to make the best of a bad situation, I began to think of ways to put a positive spin on this development. Putting my bicycle in storage was traumatic (I had been riding it until recently when my daughter-in-law, a nurse, cautioned me about broken limbs), but taking long walks in the park was equally beneficial. Husband and I met other elderly couples also concerned with keeping their hearts and lungs in good repair as we walked along, and we made friends. We hung out at the library, we went to movies and we packed lunches for our drives in the country. But, wasn't something missing? What about my legacy for the grandchildren? Had my life been of any value? Had I accomplished anything? By now surely I was wiser and had learned something to pass on to my fellow man.

I never wrote a best seller, I never found a cure for cancer, and I certainly don't have a clue why bad things happen to good people. But I do know that I have been extremely blessed – with a wonderful family, with good friends and with amazing opportunities to travel abroad. Our lives are a journey, and as we travel along we should certainly enjoy the view. Each day is a gift with endless possibilities, and I wouldn't go back to my youth with all its uncertainties for anything.

AS OLD AS YOU FEEL

You're all familiar with the expression, "You're as old as you feel," I'm sure, and there is a lot of truth in it. It applies primarily to old age but not always. As one in their latter eighties, I can tell you that in my case it often applies to which day it is. Some days I feel like hopping out of bed and tackling the clutter accumulated in the house and other days I'd just as soon stay in bed.

My youthful vim and vigor have been shot down by various ailments and health problems, which I attribute to age, but somewhere in the recesses of my mind there is a thirty or forty-year-old struggling to express herself. My brain tells me that I have stories to write, places to be and things to do. However, some days, the old body kicks in and says, "Not today, old girl; you're not up to it." With my determination, I just shelve the idea and put it off until another day; I refuse to give it up.

After a three-month period of suffering from what the doctors thought could be polymyalgia-rheumatica and scarcely being able to get out of bed, I have recently greatly improved. In fact, I just returned from a trip to the Gulf Coast and didn't miss a beat.

Once again I'm sitting at my computer writing stories, and if anyone offered a trip to Palm Springs or Nassau, you better believe I would start packing. Being blessed with the travel gene, I would probably have to be on my last legs before I'd refuse a trip most anywhere.

I've met people in their late forties and early fifties who classified themselves as "old." They even looked old. I realize that a hard life takes its toll, but I also believe it's a matter of inner resolve and determination. The bottom line is NEVER GIVE UP!!

DON'T PATRONIZE US

Nothing irritates me more than to have someone patronize me as though I were either retarded or a young child. I know I am old and look every day of my age, but when, for example, I walk in a shop and the proprietor says, "Come right in, young lady," I am tempted to turn around and walk right out. It has been seventy years since I was a "young lady" and if flattery was intended, it failed miserably.

I certainly like to be treated with respect, but who doesn't? If a handsome young man holds the door for me or gives up his seat in a waiting room, I appreciate that for I know he is a well-brought-up gentleman and would do the same for a lady whether she is thirty-five or eighty-five. But it is when a perfect stranger grabs my arm to help me up a stairway, when I have given no clue that I am helpless, that I jerk my arm back and say, "No thanks, I can manage." They may mean well but it is so condescending to those of us who face life's every challenge.

I don't consider it flattering when people feign surprise over my desire to write stories or entertain with a five course meal or baby-sit our young grandson. "What! You baby-sit (or write) at your age," they exclaim. "You should be taking life easy and letting others wait on you."

Absolutely not! If you want to hurry a senior citizen to early dementia or their grave, just take all incentive to live life normally away from them. Luckily, our son and daughter expect me to perform almost as well as they do, and that's what keeps me young at heart. Writing, keeping up with current affairs and trekking to the library every week for books to read keeps my brain stimulated while chasing my grandson provides all the exercise I could possibly need.

I am well aware that with old age comes some limitations, but if I need help when out publicly, I am not above asking for it. For example, when pushing my husband in his wheel chair, I don't hesitate to ask a stranger if they would mind holding a door for me. It's just that although up in years, we still have our pride and it's so important to continue to live an active life as long as we possibly can. Just please don't patronize us.

PERPETUALLY YOUNG

I have a dear friend, whom I shall call Martha for privacy reasons, who is the personification of this title – perpetually young. I have known her for thirty years and it seems to me that during all that time, she has scarcely aged at all. She could pass for at least twenty years younger than her eighty-six years. Could it be that she has discovered the Fountain of Youth, which Ponce de Leon searched for so valiantly? If so, I wish she would share this knowledge with yours truly. Although I am one year older than she, believe me, I look every day of my age!

Although Martha is petite in stature, she is the most energetic person I know. She is so active in community and church activities that I can hardly keep up with her schedule. She was a former first grade teacher but after retirement, she purchased a pretty home on a lake and paid for it through her own resources, determination and hard work. With her looks and personality, she certainly could have married, but it was her decision to remain single to look after her aging parents and siblings.

During a recent visit we discussed several things I had been curious about. No, she does not dye her hair; it is a beautiful burnished brown, naturally wavy with only a hint of gray in the temples. Her skin is without wrinkles and her eyes the same lively hazel as thirty years ago while her posture is straight and erect. So what is her secret? For one thing, she believes in natural remedies for the few complaints she does have. For example, she takes pineapple juice for indigestion and avoids prescription drugs as much as possible. She practices Yoga and taught it until recently. She has always enjoyed being outdoors and working in her garden and flower beds. Martha is a Master Gardner and her flowers and vegetables flourish. She cans her own vegetables and fruits and during the fall season she has a booth at the local craft fairs where she sells her delicious fig and pear preserves.

Notwithstanding all of the above, there is another factor even more telling. It is Martha's positive attitude and Christian faith. Always upbeat and reassuring, she believes in coming to the aid of anyone (human or animal) in need of assistance. When she heard at her prayer group that a homeless lady needed a place to stay, who came forward and offered shelter? Martha did, of course, and fifteen years later, this lady is happily still with her. When someone finds a dog or cat needing a "forever" home, Martha welcomes them. Her home is filled with pets and she also boards animals for a minimum of the cost a veterinarian would charge.

What a resourceful and inspiring lady! Martha surely deserves all the blessings God has bestowed on her.

AGE GIVEAWAYS

I certainly don't fault any woman or man who cares about their looks and wants to look as good as possible, especially those who are in the entertainment business. But when it comes to resorting to face-lifts, Botox injections, face abrasions and other such means, I'll pass, thank you. Every line and wrinkle on my face was shaped by Father Time, and in my opinion is a badge of honor.

Have you ever met up with a friend or relative you haven't seen in awhile and were shocked to see such a change in his/her appearance that you almost didn't recognize them? Well, I have; then I looked closer and saw the stretched skin across their cheek-bones and realized they had recently had a face lift. It was summer and the temperature in the 90's, but the inevitable scarf was wound tightly around the neck. Why? Because the flab on the neck is a dead giveaway. It's called turkey-neck. The droopy eye-lids can be lifted and lines filled in by Botox but it's not often one sees cosmetic surgery done on the neck. Our hands are another age giveaway. As the birthdays mount up, the skin on our hands becomes paper-thin and every vein protrudes. Moisturizing creams are helpful but other than wearing gloves in public, the tell-tale signs are there for all to see.

There are obviously many options out there to appeal to women's as well as men's vanity. The journals and magazines are full of advertisements for ointment, creams and procedures guaranteed to erase the signs of aging, but the only thing I smear on my face is a moisturizing cream, a dab of lipstick and a little powder, and I'm good to go. Of course in case of accidents or facial injuries, surgery is not an option but a necessity and even then not always successful, but I'm talking about elective procedures. To me there is nothing more beautiful than the natural look that Mother Nature gave us. Our character is written on our faces. The deep lines around our mouths reflect our life's joys and sense of humor; the furrows in our brows portray our serious nature – our deep thoughts and sorrows. The following poem expresses my thought.

FATHER TIME

When I was twenty I would scoff

and say that age was a long way off.

For I didn't know life's fleeting ways

quickly consumed youth's precious days.

But finally Age caught up with me.

The signs are here for all to see.

Like the river's waters silently flow,

the days did pass—and come and go.

The sorrows and joys etched each line

on a face designed by Father Time.

AGE GIVEAWAYS

Sometimes I think he wasn't too kind.
But I wrote the book; I wrote the rhyme.
So who's complaining—surely not me.
For I'm as thankful as I can be.
My visions fair, my mind is sound
and best of all, I'm still around.

TO DYE OR NOT TO DYE

To dye or not dye? Several years ago this became a difficult decision for me. I had grown older and not so caught up on my appearance so I decided it was time to let nature take its course.

I had been coloring my hair for more than twenty years and I was tired of the mess of applying the sticky dye on my head. There were certainly better things I could do with the time spent on appeasing my vanity, I thought. Most all of my acquaintances of similar age and younger simply go to the beauty shop every week and get their beauticians to color their hair, but when I learned how much they paid, I made the decision years ago to make it a home procedure and save the money. So, after getting approval from my husband, who is a most agreeable man by nature, I decided it was time to look like the white-haired Grandma I had become.

It wasn't an easy process letting the color grow out, but after several months it finally did and I had a beautiful (I thought) head of snow white hair. I called it platinum blonde. I certainly had reached that senior stage of life when according to the laws of nature, people should expect me to have white hair, but friends and family were not accustomed to seeing me *au naturel* and seemed rather shocked at the change.

Nevertheless, I stuck with my decision. The freedom of stepping in the shower and shampooing my hair without the following time-consuming procedure of applying color suited me just fine. Of course I got comments regarding my snow-white head of hair. Some of the more polite ones told me, "It provides a soft frame for your face" while others were more direct, "It makes you look your age," they said. That's okay, I thought. I am as old as I am and letting my hair go white is just being natural.

Well, that was then. With my next birthday practically coinciding with the annual family reunion, I took a good, hard look at myself in the mirror the other day and thought: *I'm really looking old. I should do something to improve my appearance. Wouldn't it be fun to surprise the relatives and attend the family reunion this year as a blonde?* So… what did I do today? I went to the beauty shop and consulted the beautician. She suggested a color rinse that would shampoo out. It turned out a nice reddish-blonde and took at least ten years off my age! This is something I can easily do at home, and who knows – I may have to experiment with some of the other shades this product offers. My husband definitely approves.

WE ALL HAVE A STORY

Okay, you've finally reached the point in your life that for years you've been looking forward to – you've retired! At last you can do all the things you didn't have time for. You sleep late, you read, you travel, you meet friends for coffee, and you watch a lot of TV. But, suddenly you feel bored. What now? I have the answer which proved to be one of the most rewarding things I've ever done: Write your memoirs.

I can hear you now. You're saying, "But I've lived a dull, ordinary life. I didn't have an impoverished youth. Nothing dramatic ever happened to me." Wrong! We all have a story. It will be a legacy for your grandchildren and for generations to come. Your friends will have more insight into the person you are and they will love it. In fact, by the time I started going down memory lane (in my eighties) and reminiscing about my life, I found a flood of memories coming back. I couldn't get my thoughts down on paper fast enough.

Here are some pointers I found helpful when I sat down and began to write:

- Begin your story with an amusing or momentous incident. It will catch the reader's interest. Don't make it an autobiography. There's nothing more boring than a story that begins: I was born in such and such a year in such and such a place. You want to write about segments from your life but not necessarily in chronological order.

- Write about your first love, your first job or your first day in school. Write about the fascinating people you've known who have made an impact on your life. You may want to include a chapter on your faith and how it has sustained you through difficult times. And much more!

- Be truthful. Don't try to embellish your story. We've all had disappointments and regrets. It makes us more human to include some of the things we've endured. But don't be modest, either. Above all, don't leave out your accomplishments.
- Fill your story with vivid descriptions. Use all your senses – sight, sound, smells. For example, "The prairie wind howled a plaintive whistle under my front door."

When you finish you will have a fresh understanding of your life – how each part of it shaped you into the person you are. It will help you make sense of your life and you will find that writing from memory sharpens your intellect as well. Now you are ready to take your story to your local printer and have them print and bind it. Then at your next family reunion hand out a copy to each one of your relatives. You may find that they even want you to autograph your little book of memoirs. Enjoy. Don't we all deserve to achieve a small measure of immortality?

Mary with her publisher, Cheryl Haynes

PURSUE A HOBBY

Everyone should have a hobby. If you're like me, I participated actively in mine during mid-life but have let it slip by the wayside during my senior years. Whether it's painting, collecting vintage post cards, woodworking, bird watching, scrapbooking or whatever, it's more important now than ever to renew our interest in whatever we were once passionate about. Mine were dolls and I have a room upstairs full of them lacking attention. I have always loved dolls and still have a baby doll Santa brought me when I was seven years old. She is being displayed in an antique wicker carriage in the doll room. However, in the seventies I became interested in the making of applehead dolls and needing a source of supplementing our income, I learned the art of making them and attended hundreds of craft fairs selling these little grandma and grandpa dolls. I dressed them in old-fashioned dresses or overalls and often displayed them sitting in a miniature rocking chair holding a little Bible or on a stand. Especially around the time of the bicentennial in 1976, they sold like hot cakes. From this extra income I was not only able to contribute to household expenses but with my savings, I was able to take my family to Paris in 1979.

PURSUE A HOBBY

Mary's daughter, Julianne with Applehead Dolls, 1973

At one of the craft fairs, I spotted a lady with the most beautiful dolls I had ever seen. They were reproductions of antique French and German dolls from the late 1800's or early 1900's. I was so fascinated I couldn't stay away from her booth. It was then I determined that if I ever had the money, I would purchase an original antique bisque doll.

PURSUE A HOBBY

Over the years, I was fortunate enough to buy several German dolls such as Armand Marseille, Simon & Halbig and Kestner, but I was never financially able to purchase a French doll, such as Jumeau or Bru. These were incredibly expensive and have gained in value each year since then. Over the years, I was able to add to my collection with American dolls as well, such as an original Shirley Temple. I joined a doll club and thoroughly enjoyed attending meetings once a month with others sharing their knowledge of various dolls. It was a fascinating science, determining the maker and authenticity of antique dolls.

If you've never had a hobby, now is the time to decide what interests you and pursue it; if you've let yours slip by the wayside, as I have, let's do something about it. As we grow older, we need to indulge ourselves with things we enjoy and keep our minds occupied as much as possible. I think I'll look up that doll club tomorrow.

CAT COMPANY/DOG COMPANY

My family and I have always been cat lovers although we've had our share of dogs, also, who were like members of the family. However, now that Gene and I are octogenarians and afflicted with arthritis, cats seem the wiser choice for us. Cats adapt well to litter boxes rather than needing frequent outdoor excursions to relieve themselves and never have to be taken on walks.

When Finley, our last cat, passed on to kitty heaven last fall, we were so heart-broken it was months before we could even think of getting another one. The house began to seem devoid of that extra little four-footed personality and knowing that we felt a bit lonely, our daughter prevailed on us to visit one of the local cat rescue facilities. When we told the lady in charge how much Gene enjoyed Finley, who was his lap companion, she disappeared in the rear of the facility and brought out a beautiful Lynx-point tabby named Sassy. She then asked Gene to have a seat in the rocking chair, and to our amazement, Sassy immediately jumped up in his lap. We were sold.

Mitzi

The first thing we did was re-name her. She has such a calm, sweet disposition, that "Sassy" did not suit this two year-old kitty at all. After a few days' deliberation, she was renamed Mitzi. She continues to be great company for us and spends much of her day curled up in Gene's lap. She gives us both so much pleasure.

Another point in favor of cats is when you hear a noise at night, you can pass it off as "it's probably the cat" and go on back to sleep. However, this brings to mind an occurrence some years ago when we lived in Whitehaven and burglary became a real issue in the neighborhood. Approaching mid-night one evening, my husband, son, daughter and I heard a loud crash somewhere in the opposite side of the house. Positive that we had a burglar breaking in, we all four skittered to the front bedroom, locked the door and called the police. After what seemed an eternity, the police arrived and did a thorough search of the shrubs around the house before coming inside. What did they find but a potted plant knocked off a table on the entry way from the carport and broken in little pieces. Sitting nearby was Boots the cat. Were we ever embarrassed!

So… bottom line: if you're feeling a bit lonely and need good company – get a cat. Odd noises at night need not bother you. It's probably the cat!

YEARNING TO TRAVEL

Frances Mayes said it best in her book, *A YEAR IN THE WORLD*: "The need to travel is a mysterious force. A desire to go runs through me equally with an intense desire to stay at home. An equal and opposite thermodynamic principle. When I travel I think of home and what it means. At home I'm dreaming of catching trains at night in the gray light of Old Europe, or pushing open shutters to see Florence awaken. The balance just slightly tips in the direction of the airport."

I love my home and am always happy to return to it safely after a journey abroad or across the U.S., but after a few weeks, housework loses its appeal, and like Frances Mayes, I'm ready to be off and away somewhere again. I begin thinking I haven't been to Cancun or Yosemite National Park or some other destination, and I'm ready to start packing. My husband is blessed with a very practical, easy disposition and is equally content to stay home or go places with me; however, it's obvious that our children have caught the "travel bug" from me.

    Our son is home scarcely a few weeks from one trip until he is off to some foreign country again. He just returned from the Czech Republic, Holland, Germany and Austria and he now leaves in two weeks on a medical mission trip to Nigeria. Many prayers go with him as he often travels to politically unstable countries, but I know that he is never happier than to do so. Our daughter, like me, exists looking forward to her next excursion.

    Maybe it is genetic – my yearning to see more of this beautiful world in which we live. Certainly my father enjoyed exploring new places and liked to always be on the move. I remember him saying, "You shouldn't live in one place more than two years; if you do, you stagnate." That may be a little extreme, but I know there was nothing he enjoyed more than seeing new places.

I wouldn't take anything for the trips I've been so fortunate to make, both overseas and in this country, or to quote St. Augustine, "The world is a book and those who do not travel read only a page." It's always a learning experience and has made me a more accepting person of those of other beliefs and cultures. I realize that foreign travel at my stage in life is now greatly curtailed, but just suggest a trip to Nassau or Palm Beach, and I'll start packing tonight.

Mary and Gene taking a gondola ride in Venice

PIPE DREAMS

While lying in bed this morning, I had a disturbing thought: Even if I won the lottery, I wouldn't be physically able to do much with it at my age – like travel to exotic places all over the world, such as Tahiti and Istanbul, or own a vacation home on a Caribbean island with that azure blue water extending out to the horizon. Even five years ago, I probably would have cashed that multi-million dollar check and realized such far-fetched dreams, but arthritis and various health problems have surfaced since then, preventing any thoughts of long distance travels or buying idyllic vacation homes.

Of course there are good things I could still do with such riches, such as help relatives with financial problems, benefit various philanthropic organizations and set up trust funds for the grandchildren. My church and pastor would certainly not be forgotten either. I wouldn't want a larger home for I can scarcely maintain this one and having servants would only disturb me. Well, okay, I might as well admit I just might want to buy a new car – say a Porsche or Lamborghini (if I could get into it).

Pipe dreams aside, I have so much to be thankful for without the headaches that accompany such wealth. I have traveled to most of the European countries as well as to Canada, Hawaii and Mexico and many of the Caribbean islands. I still have my sweet husband and our house is paid for. And we have two wonderful children and three of the smartest, most handsome grandsons in the world! What else could I wish for? Oh, good health, of course. But that is something money can't buy.

SAY WHAT?

Several years ago when my husband began losing some hearing, I'm afraid I was not as sympathetic as I should have been. He would think I said the craziest things, like one day I said, "I've lost my easel." Gene replied, "What do you want with a weasel?" Sometimes it gave me a laugh but at other times, it was annoying. I urged him to get a hearing aid, but he would have no part of that.

Contrary to Gene, I was in hearing loss denial at first. I was sure he had started whispering when he spoke to me. He has always been soft-spoken, and is physically unable to raise his voice even a decibel or two without sounding hoarse and angry. But since a lot of other people began to be unintelligible, I finally faced up to the fact that the problem was not theirs or Gene's – but, mine.

It seems that within a few months, I had lost most of the hearing in my left ear and the right one is going fast. The shoe was now definitely on the other foot, so to speak. When something I say comes across as total gibberish, Gene doesn't laugh; he just asks me to repeat what I said. Across the room his words are totally non-decipherable to me, but I have found that sitting across the table from each other at meal time, we communicate just fine. We have started lingering over our meals so that we can have a real conversation.

Now even when visitors pop in, I scurry to make a pot of coffee so that we can gather around the dining room table in order for me to hear what is being said. Strangely enough, Gene doesn't seem to need this proximity to be able to carry on a conversation. Could it be that he never had a real hearing problem or that his hearing has improved? Either way, I'm thankful he seems better. As for me, I keep putting off that appointment with the audiologist. I'm not crazy about the idea of wearing a hearing aid, but I have to realize that it's just another part of the aging process... but, thankfully, one with a solution.

ONE OF LIFE'S TRIALS

Without doubt, the foremost trial of growing older is health-related. Few of us escape without having some sort of problems…some serious and some not.

As for me, I nearly died of double pneumonia as a baby and remained frail until well in my teens. I remember my father telling me that when (and if) I ever married, I should never have children. He didn't believe that I was strong enough. Well, I proved him wrong. I married and had not one but two beautiful babies. I made it fine.

During my life, it hasn't been all "a bed of roses," by any means, but enough bumps in the road, so to speak, to make me most thankful and grateful for the smooth ones. I've had my share of surgeries and my body is criss-crossed with the scars left by stitches to prove it. None of the laparoscopic surgery would work on me so the surgeon's scalpel was the instrument in use on each occasion. Few thought at my age I would live through the last surgery a couple of years ago, but I surprised them. I remember the anesthesiologist pushing me to the surgery and stopping to ask if I would mind if he said a prayer before we went in. Of course I wouldn't mind; I would be most appreciative, I told him. He proceeded to say a beautiful prayer and I went in calm and relaxed, assured that God was in control. The surgery went fine.

This old body has succumbed to arthritis during the last decade, and periodically I get nerve "blocks" when the pain gets too severe. I went through an especially debilitating spell this past spring. The doctors were puzzled about the severity of my symptoms but finally came up with a name: polymyalgia-rheumatica. Unfortunately, the treatment was rather obscure and not really advisable, so I decided to ride it out. I'm happy to report that with warm weather, it gradually subsided.

With each episode of health problems, I give credit to prayer and devout Christian physicians for my recovery. I believe that this is why I am here today – living, breathing and enjoying the multitude of joy that comes with each waking moment.

ACCOLADES TO OUR DOCTORS

I sometimes think that husband and I would have very little social life if we didn't visit our doctors so frequently. It seems like hardly a week passes that either he or I don't see our internal medicine physician or a specialist in one field or another.

When we first started housekeeping, there was a doctor in Whitehaven who was adept not only in family practice but in most any field of medicine. He was "on call" night and day, and he made house calls when one of us was too sick to get out of bed—something almost unheard of today. He didn't hesitate to do some surgery, when needed, and I'm sure I would have trusted him to deliver my first child if he had agreed.

I'll never forget his stock comment after hearing our complaints. He would say, "I'll give you a little medicine and you'll soon feel better." And we always did. He has passed on to his rewards a good many years ago, but his name is legend in that part of town.

Now we not only have an internal medicine physician but we see specialists in urology, arthritis, dermatology, surgery, podiatry, ophthalmology and even a pain specialist for my occasional bouts of spinal stenosis. However, it is my dentist who deserves special appreciation. He puts up with my abnormal fears and does his best to pacify me. No paraphernalia in my mouth – not even a cotton roll. How he works around all this is beyond me, but he's good.

Without this bevy of doctors, several amazing surgeons and much prayer, I'm sure I would never have reached these senior years. It involves a daily regimen of pills – so many that I can scarcely keep up with all of them, but with the aid of these prescribed drugs, frequent visits to the doctors, diagnostic tests and many supplications to our Lord and Savior, my husband and I are still alive and kicking.

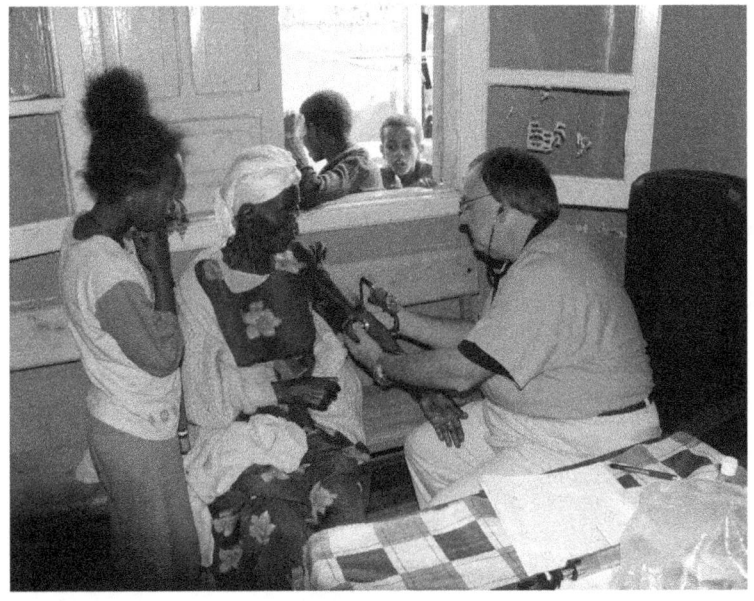

Mary's son, Dr. Gene Scobey on a mission in Ethiopia

Accolades to all these men and women who have dedicated their lives to keeping us healthy. I know how hard they work and how dedicated they are for our son is one of them.

A SIGNIFICANT ANNIVERSARY

Sixty years ago I married one of the finest men on God's earth. Those years have passed all too quickly. I realize that couples celebrating their Diamond Anniversary are few and far between, and I'm so thankful that we have been able to reach this milestone in our lives.

It was a foggy night the last of January, 1953, when this handsome young man came to my door on a blind date after a mutual friend suggested that we should meet. I was impressed from the beginning that here was a man with all the courtesies and manners of a well-brought-up Southern gentleman, and I was anxious to see him again. We began to date regularly and soon found out that we had much in common. We were both from small towns in Mississippi, and, in fact, were born in adjoining counties. We shared the same faith and the same values and were both graduates of "Ole Miss" (the University of Mississippi).

The chances of us ever meeting were pretty slim. We never knew each other while in college even though several friends told me about him and thought that we should meet. After graduation, I moved with my parents to Kansas, where I taught my first year of school in a one-room school out on the prairie. The harsh climate soon drove us back to the South, and we settled in Memphis where I took a teaching position. It was one of my fellow teachers who managed the introduction and after a whirlwind courtship we were married six months later.

These sixty years have been wonderful years. I thank God for bringing us together for I know that our destiny has always been in His hands.

A SIGNIFICANT ANNIVERSARY

Mary and Gene Scobey

THE FAMILY REUNION

Almost seventy years ago it became a tradition in our family to get together for a reunion each September. It is an event that each of us look forward to from one year to the next. In the beginning there were our grandparents, parents and relatives from as far away as Montana who attended, but as the years passed and our parents and grandparents passed away, it became my generation who organized the event.

I'll never forget the wonderful food that was prepared for the Sunday picnics before returning home each year. Our mothers, aunts and cousins were always outstanding cooks and each tried to prepare something special to serve. The desserts

THE FAMILY REUNION

were amazing and drew the ultimate compliments as well as requests to share the recipes.

Originally, we met at state parks where each family had their individual cabin with kitchens, so some of the meals could be prepared there, but for the last ten years the present generation decided to make it easy on ourselves by reserving rooms at the lodge and eating at the restaurant there. Not having to bother with carrying groceries to our retreat was a vast improvement in my thinking, although I do miss the tasty dishes my relatives used to prepare.

It has been interesting to see the changes that the years have wrought in our reunion attendance. Now my generation is comprised by those of us in our seventies and eighties with our children and grandchildren attending. We come from the tri-state area and in most cases, have not seen each other since the previous September. Each year the grandchildren seemed to have changed the most while some of us seniors have

THE FAMILY REUNION

developed health issues. This year one member was in a wheelchair and another was too ill to attend. However, a precious four-month old baby, who is my great-great niece, was brought by her parents, and I loved having her little hand curl around my finger as I exclaimed over her. Such is the progression of generations in each family, all of whom are very dear to me. Meeting together for our family reunion each year fosters closeness and bonding and is certainly a tradition I hope the younger generations will carry on.

Ashmore Family Reunion

LOST IN CYBER SPACE

I am definitely of the opinion that technology in communication is getting totally out of control. First, the telephone system a la Alexander Graham Bell spun off with AT&T, Verizon and now U-Verse, to name a few. Then the cellular phone came to prominence in the nineties and now seems to be rapidly taking the place of home phones. Technology is changing so fast it makes my head spin!

I valiantly fought against joining forces with the cyber space addicts. This old woman has trouble enough getting the TV to behave, but lo and behold, my son appeared on my door steps some five or six years ago with a computer he was discarding in favor of a more sophisticated machine with the declaration that it would be invaluable to this aged mother who liked to write stories. I assured him that not being mechanically inclined, I would NEVER learn how to operate it... so guess who is sitting at her desk right now typing away on her PC? Joining the throngs surfing the WEB, blogging, sending e-mails or "googling" for information was beyond my wildest imagination, but each have become almost common-place. And even more astonishing, I am now an advocate of Facebook! How else would I keep up with the shenanigans of my grandsons?

    For a while the Blackberry, a multi-tasking apparatus, seemed to be the next replacement for cell phones, but now there are iPhones, iPads, iPods and others. SKYPE, in which you can view the person with whom you are speaking, is where I draw the line. No one needs to see this grandma in everyday attire – usually still in her housecoat with rollers in her hair.

LOST IN CYBER SPACE

All of this technology has bred a new language, such as "Do you twitter?" No, I do not nor am I likely to. My grandsons talk about downloading music to their iPods. A while back one of them bragged on Facebook that he had just bought an iPhone 5. His brother replied, "Why not wait for the iPhone 6?" I didn't have a clue what they were talking about. They might as well have been speaking a foreign language.

For some time GPS has been available on aircraft, ships and automobiles but now you can get GPS on cell phones. A device called a Kindle wirelessly downloads books from the internet through wi-fi or through a computer. Already I have heard of the closing of two booksellers in town while libraries are attempting to meet the demands by making material for e-book readers available. I understand that text books in schools will soon be obsolete. I cringe to think our way of life is beginning to be affected to this extent.

Technology in communications is changing so fast that what's "in" today is outdated tomorrow. As for me, I'm ready to declare a "status quo".

Well, okay. If Santa decides to slip a Kindle in my stocking this Christmas, I might be prevailed on to accept—just this one little exception, of course. I do love to read.

Mary at her desk

SIMPLE PLEASURES

It's the simple pleasures in life that bring me out of bed each morning, excited to see what the day brings. Big occasions are pretty rare, but if we stop and think about it, simple pleasures abound every day in each of our lives. For example, here are some of mine:

1. The smell of coffee my dear husband has perking away in the kitchen by the time I am up. It gets us both started on our day.
2. Reading a good book.
3. Seeing a rainbow after a stormy afternoon.
4. The sound of soft rain drops pattering on the sky light, lulling me to sleep.

5. Picking figs from our back yard fig bush.
6. Eating a sandwich for lunch made from a fresh, garden tomato.
7. Husband and I sitting on the patio in early evening and listening to the birds up in the trees "tweeting" their lullabies.
8. A drop-in visit from a neighbor. Good neighbors are such a blessing.
9. Hugs from our five-year-old grandson after a visit to their house or a visit to ours.
10. Daily calls and frequent visits from our precious daughter. What would we do without her!
11. Our kitty cat, Mitzi, sleeping at the foot of our bed. She hardly stirs all night.

12. Watching "Wheel of Fortune" with my sweet husband each evening (except Sundays, of course).
13. A call from a friend or relative I haven't heard from in a while. The time flies by while we catch up on news.
14. Our dear son taking time from his busy schedule as a physician to show us slides from his most recent medical mission trip.
15. A call from our wonderful son-in-law, inviting us to dinner. He's a great cook.
16. Looking through old picture albums. Oh, the memories they bring back!
17. Christmas morning brunches our amazing daughter-in-law always prepares. We look forward to her specialties: cheese grits, eggs and

sausage casserole and coffee cake – so yummy!

18. E-mails from our two older grandsons – both of whom are now four hundred miles away in college at UT-Knoxville.

19. Reading old love letters my father wrote to my mother before they married in 1920. (Yes, I keep everything.)

There are more, of course, but you get the idea. What are your simple pleasures?

PAY IT FORWARD

Recently my husband and I were treating ourselves to breakfast at the Waffle house and had almost completed our meals, when a nice looking man, who had been sitting on one of the stools nearby, approached us and said, "I took care of your ticket." Gene and I were so astonished that we barely mumbled a "thank you" before he turned and left the establishment.

We stared at each other and said, "What was that all about?" Never before had either of us in our entire lives had a stranger pay for our meals. Did we look so impoverished that he felt sorry for us? Or was it because we were old? We were appreciative, of course, but couldn't help mulling over the reasons for his selecting us to bestow such an act of kindness.

I was well aware of the title of the book, *Pay It Forward*, by Catherine Ryan Hyde and even saw the movie by that name. It is based on the premise that each person can make a difference by taking the time to show love and kindness to the people around them. Was that what this was all about?

When we got home, I couldn't wait to get on the computer and find out more about this intriguing thought. I learned that the term "pay it forward" suggests that the beneficiary of a good deed should repay it to others instead of the original benefactor. This idea is not new. In fact, this was a key element in a Greek play, *Dyskolos*, in 317 BC!

When I told our daughter about this incident, she agreed that the man was "paying it forward" for some good deed he had received. In fact, she said that there is a recent trend to designate Fridays as "Pay it Forward Friday." And, yes, it was on

Friday when our incident occurred. Mystery solved. Now I can't wait to repay this man's kind act to someone else.

RETIREMENT

RETIREMENT

The word, retirement, means different things to different people. There are some who have looked forward to it for years. They can't wait to be free of a daily schedule and having to be at work at a certain time each morning. They look forward to being able to travel and pursue hobbies they have put on hold for  years. Then there are others who dread it. They can see only boring days ahead with little purpose in life. They feel "put out to pasture."

Some companies have a hard and fast rule that all employees must retire at sixty-five with the

RETIREMENT

option of taking early retirement at sixty-two. Others allow their employees to work well past those years as long as their work is up to par.

My husband worked as an accountant until he was seventy-two and even fifteen years later regrets being unemployed. Although he suffers from arthritis and walks with a walker indoors, his mind is as sharp as ever. It has become my job to help plan activities to get him out of the house and make sure he doesn't get depressed. So far, so good.

There are some who looked forward to retirement but found it lacking in fulfillment. In the beginning they traveled to foreign countries, took cruises and took part in a whirlwind of social activities, but as their health declined, they fell prey to depression.

As for me, I have the perfect solution – work part time. As a counselor for a foreign student exchange program I helped found in 1981, I wait until I am consulted to call students with problems and write my reports. I certainly would not want the confinement of an eight- to- five job.

I admire a friend of ours who faced retirement with the most positive attitude possible. As an avid golfer, he couldn't wait to "hit the greens" as often as possible after he retired and not only is he President of the local Kiwanis Club but he works with Alliance for the Blind and Vision Impaired, attends weekly Bible study with senior citizens and teaches adults to read one day a week...and one day a week teaches adults to read.

His days are so filled with activities, he scarcely has time to get bored. He is an example to all of us – keep busy as long as possible.

THE CYCLE OF LIFE

As William Shakespeare put it, "One man in his life plays many parts. His acts being seven ages." Thus, it seems to me that my husband and I are somewhere between the sixth and seventh acts. We are, no doubt, in our second childhood, but, luckily, still have our sight, most of our teeth and food still tastes pretty good.

I have lived to witness six generations on my maternal side, beginning with my great grandmother, who lived to be one hundred and two, my grandmother, my mother and then there is me. Our son and his wife came next, producing two handsome grandsons. They represent the fifth and sixth generations. But nothing has made me more aware of the cycle of life then the birth of an adorable baby boy to our daughter and her husband over five years ago – little William.

Our son's two boys are now young men, each occupied with their own interests, so what a delight it has been to watch little William progress from infancy to an inquisitive little boy, so busy he scarcely has time to succumb to sleep. Each day he amazes me with his grasp of new words and the ability to communicate. When a word he searches for (to express a thought) fails him, in frustration he has been known to flatten himself on the floor in tears. But when he asks for me to do something and follows it with "please, Grandmother," it's impossible to refuse. After all, isn't that the prerogative of a grandparent to spoil a grandchild?

When I look at William and think of all the genetic factors involved in the creation of this little personality. It gives me a sharp awareness of all the generations before him and all the lives that preceded him – perhaps his inquisitive nature from "Uncle G," his love of music from his father and paternal grandparents, his artistic ability from his mother and who knows from how far back other traits have evolved. In looks, the small up-turned nose must surely come from my husband's side of the family, but those big, blue eyes are definitely from his father's side.

With his little hand in mine, William and I take walks, and he stops to gather some pretty pebbles or watch with delight as a squirrel jumps from limb to limb of a tree. He is an explorer, discovering all the delights of the world in which we live and making me more aware of the beauty in small things that I had long taken for granted. He is all boy. Our daughter's doll house is no longer inhabited by small dolls but by little cars.

Perhaps, according to Mr. Shakespeare, my husband and I have reverted to the second or third stages of our lives. We both sit on the floor and work in pieces to a puzzle or build Lego Skyscrapers with young William. This should certainly indicate that we are enjoying our second childhood. He enhances our lives. He is unique and there is certainly no one else on earth exactly like him. Such is the cycle of life.

Grandson, William converts his mother's dollhouse into a garage

Three Generations

BLESSINGS

When I think about all the blessings in my life, I am awe-struck. There are too many to mention, so I'll just list the ones at the top of my list.

I am most blessed to still have my dear husband of sixty years. Gene is my rock, my helpmate, my friend and my love. He is the most patient, kind, devoted husband anyone could wish for. He has the most amazing memory, and I call on him frequently for dates and places I can't recall. I have so many friends who are widows and some have been for many years, and I know how lucky I am. My husband's only sibling, a brother, has been deceased for almost twenty years; yet he was the younger, athletic one. It seems that, in most cases, women are genetically geared to outlast men.

Our children and grandchildren are certainly a blessing to both of us. However, Gene and I had been married almost four years before our son was born and it was nine and a half years later before our daughter's birth. By that time, I was in my early forties and had given up hope that we would ever have another child. What a wonderful surprise! Our son was an active, busy child who kept us both hopping while our daughter was (and still is) very serene and calm. Both have been amazing achievers and make us so proud. We have been blessed with three grandsons, who are such a joy to us. Like most grandparents, we think they are the most handsome, intelligent boys on earth.

Our minister is one in a million! What would we do without his inspiring sermons? I will never cease to be grateful for his visits while I was in the hospital and the Sunday he read from

BLESSINGS

one of my books to the congregation. He is certainly a blessing in our lives.

If one is blessed with good health as they age, they are fortunate, indeed. I can't say that my husband and I have had perfect health throughout the years, by any means, but with God's blessings and the miracle of modern medicine, here we are in our late eighties, happy to wake up each morning and enjoy another day on God's beautiful earth.

William

John and Justin

MY FAITH

When I was in my early twenties and still living at home with my parents, we had an elderly neighbor who shared some of her wisdom on faith with me. It went something like this: "It doesn't matter which train we take; we're all headed for the same station." Made sense to me then…and still does.

I could never abide people who are so dogmatic that they can't tolerate other faiths besides their own. They will tell you that if you don't belong to their particular church, you are headed for Hell. What slander and ignorance! As long as you are Christian, does it really matter if you are Baptist, Methodist, Presbyterian, Catholic or whatever? I don't think so.

MY FAITH

My parents were Baptists but did not attend services very often except on special occasions, such as weddings, funerals and occasionally revivals. We had a large family Bible in the house and Dad gave an impressive blessing before meals, but I don't think they considered church attendance as having much correlation with being Christians.

Dad's work necessitated that we move around a lot, but when we finally settled down for a few years in a small North Mississippi town, I began attending G.A.'s at the First Baptist Church. During one meeting the director asked that everyone who was a Christian, raise their hand. I raised my hand. Several girls looked at me aghast and proclaimed, "You're not a Christian!" I was crushed. In my naivety, I thought if you believed in Jesus Christ and that he was your Savior, you were a Christian. I didn't know that you had to be baptized before the congregation to be a Christian and to be saved. Somehow that fact had failed to be impressed on me during my up-bringing.

After that I had several meetings with the pastor and had it all explained to me. Being immersed in water and being deathly afraid of drowning (I had never learned to swim) was something I had to pray long and hard about. So the date was set for my baptism. I made it fine. Now I had been obedient to His command and could truthfully proclaim that I was a Christian.

At that time, I was fourteen years old, and wrote the following poem:

I GIVE MY SOUL TO JESUS

I give my soul to Jesus and hope he'll take it, too; Of course the world is fine but when my life is through,

I'll be waiting for the angel all dressed in snowy white, with silvery outspread wings to take me through the night.

She'll lay me on a pillow that shines just like gold and open up her wings that had been in a fold and softly we will fly up, up into the sky where people never die.

I give my soul to Jesus and I'll never be sorry I know, for I know that up in Heaven is a wonderful place to go.

Those words are just as meaningful in my life today as they were then, I strongly believe in the value of prayer. Each day I awake with a prayer on my lips, thanking God for granting me another day on this beautiful earth and for the many blessings He has bestowed on me. I often find myself praying during the day for a sick friend or a special need someone has. I know that He hears and He answers. True, it is not always exactly what I pray for, but He, who is all-knowing, knows what is best and countless times I have come to realize that His will – not mine – turns out to be for my own good. Even until this day, I continue to be a work in progress toward being a better Christian. It is something I shall continue to do as long as I live.

Mary at age 16

SEIZE THE DAY

Everyone gets old if they live long enough. It's a fact of life. We have no control over our age. From infancy we grow older each year, and (hopefully) smarter. I remember when I was nine, saying proudly, "I'm nine going on ten." I got over that when I was around thirteen or fourteen. Twenties and thirties were pretty fine, but then I hit forty and I was "over the hill." Supposedly it's all downhill after that, but actually, that's the easy part. Going downhill always is, isn't it? In reality, that's the prime of life. When I reached my fifties and sixties, I became less open about blurting out my age, but at seventy and eighty, it's a real accomplishmentand I started bragging. Will Rogers once said, "When you stop lying about your age and start bragging, you're old." Now that I'm past the eight decade mark, I somehow manage to bring it up in conversation all the time.

The last twenty years have actually been the best part of my life. I no longer hold a regular job (just a part-time one) and can sleep as late as I like and go to bed whenever I please. I love taking advantage of senior discounts on everything from hotels to museums and theaters to dining out. And respect like I've never had before! Handsome young men rush to open doors for me or give up their seats in the waiting room. For the first time in my life I feel free to speak my mind and I don't hesitate to give advice. There's time to pursue hobbies and interests I've always wanted but put aside like writing and painting. Several magazines and papers have printed my stories and I have published two books. I also took an art class recently and now enjoy doing pastels of my grandchildren. And speaking of... I never knew I could sprint so fast until our youngest grandchild took a notion to ride his tricycle in the street while I was baby-sitting him one day. But what joy our three grandsons are!

Like most elderly, I have my share of health issues and pills to take, but each day is a gift from God. The ancient Romans had a phrase for it – "carpe diem," which translated from the Latin means "seize the day." So enjoy. Live every day in the present and make it beautiful... or as Robert Browning put it:

> Grow old along with me
> The best is yet to be.
> The last of life,
> for which the first was made

Meet the Author

Mary Ashmore Scobey was born in Lafayette County, Mississippi and proudly admits to having reached the stage of octogenarian. She received her B.A. and M.A. degrees from the University of Mississippi with majors in French and English. Mary then began a career of teaching and has been employed by the American Intercultural Student Exchange for the past thirty-two years. She and her husband reside in Cordova, Tennessee and have two children. Their son is a physician and their daughter worked as the Program Coordinator for WMC-TV until she left to be a stay-at-home mom. Mary and Gene have three grandsons who are their "pride and joy."

Writing poems and short stories have always been a favorite pastime of Mary's. She wrote her first poem at the age of eleven; got it published in the *Commercial Appeal* and has been "hooked"

MEET THE AUTHOR

ever since. She has written two books previously, *French Memoirs – World War I* and *Just Passing Through*, and has had a number of short stories published in *Reminisce, Today's Mississippi Woman, The Oxford Eagle, The Tupelo Journal, Tombigbee Country Magazine, The Oxford So & So* and various other journals and magazines. There is nothing Mary enjoys more than writing – unless it is traveling.

Mary holds a copy of her father's WWI biography.

Mary's book signing with her daughter, Juli Parks.

Mary with her publisher, Cheryl Haynes

www.ingramcontent.com/pod-product-compliance
Lightning Source LLC
Chambersburg PA
CBHW020014050426
42450CB00005B/460